The Clink
Desserts
Cookbook

All recipes by Al Crisci, unless otherwise credited

Contents

Christopher Moore
Clink Chief Executive

'Changing attitudes, transforming lives and creating second chances'

The sole aim of The Clink Charity is to reduce reoffending rates by training our graduates and placing them, upon release from prison, into employment in the hospitality industry.

Since launching the first Clink Restaurant at HMP High Down in 2009, we now have seven projects, which achieve outstanding results by offering our five-step integrated programme.

Prisoners at The Clink work a 40-hour week, simulating a professional environment. Our dedicated full-time trainers and assessors work closely with them to help them gain their City & Guilds NVQs. Upon release, support workers help our graduates to find employment and housing, then mentor them weekly, helping them reintegrate into society.

In 2016, The Clink trained up to 160 prisoners each day. Of the 92 Clink graduates released, 89 went into full-time employment and three into rehab. Between them they had gained 138 full NVQ level 2 qualifications. In November 2016, figures from the Justice Data Lab showed that prisoners going through The Clink Charity training programmes are 41% less likely to reoffend*. (Our graduates were measured comparatively against non-Clink-trained individuals who were similar in circumstance.) More than 250 employers are willing to take on our graduates, subject to interview.

We currently operate four Clink Restaurants, at HMP High Down, HMP Cardiff, HMP Brixton and HMP Styal. By dining at one of our restaurants, you're supporting the prisoners' training and giving them the experience they require. The Clink menus are created around the seasons, local produce and the City & Guilds syllabus. Each restaurant also offers facilities for corporate events and private dining.

In addition to the restaurants, we operate Clink Gardens at HMP Send and HMP High Down to achieve City & Guilds NVQs in horticulture. Fruit, vegetables and herbs from the gardens are used by the restaurants, along with eggs from our chickens.

Clink Events provides catering beyond the prison walls. It gives prisoners and homeless clients from the Centrepoint charity the chance to gain qualifications in event catering and prepare for full-time employment. We are building a central production kitchen for Clink Events and looking for future sites in UK prisons. Our aim is to see more than 1,000 highly trained Clink graduates enter employment each year by 2020.

We are proud that, with our partner HMPPS, we achieve extraordinary outcomes in a value-for-money way, while fulfilling our core values of compassion, professionalism and integrity in an environment with so many daily challenges.

We hope that The Clink demonstrates what can be achieved when society engages collectively to help those who want and deserve a second chance.

* Ministry of Justice (2016) Population and capacity briefing for Friday 17 June 2016, London: Ministry of Justice

Finlay Scott
Clink Chairman and Founder Trustee

As I write this, The Clink has four excellent restaurants, two garden projects, and an outside event catering enterprise. We have exciting plans, not only to open more restaurants, but also to continue to grow our enterprises into bakery and other craft-based industries. The whole focus of our Charity is to train prisoners in cooking, food preparation and service and then to help them into work upon leaving prison. This has, over the last seven years, produced remarkable outcomes, with the 900 trainees who have gone through our programme achieving a 90% success rate. In turn, this has led to a reduction in reoffending, with the result of less crime and fewer victims.

This is the third in our series of cookbooks. We collect recipes from our Charity ambassadors, trustees, employees and supporters, with the entire proceeds of sales going to continuing our work to reduce crime in the UK.

I hope that you enjoy the recipes in the book and, while cooking these lovely puddings, that you might remember how you are helping inmates to rehabilitate themselves. It has been found that the very act of food preparation and cooking is restorative for our inmates, as well as giving them a skill that they can use to re-enter society upon their release from prison.

Bon Appétit!

Simple

Lemon curd ice cream
Sheila Dillon, Food Programme, BBC Radio 4

Makes about 1 litre

Ingredients

1 unwaxed or organic lemon
600ml double cream (the best
   you can find)
320g jar of the best lemon curd
   (only buy the stuff with just
   4 ingredients: butter,
   lemons, sugar, eggs)

Method

Zest the lemon with a fine-toothed grater. Squeeze out the lemon juice.

Whip the cream to soft peaks. Fold in the lemon curd and the lemon zest. Then taste it: if it needs a little more sharpness, fold in some lemon juice... carefully, and tasting as you go. Put it in a freezable container and freeze until firm; there's no need to stir it during the freezing process.

Serve with brandy snaps or shortbread, or crushed raspberries. Or just eat it on its own.

Raspberry and limoncello trifle
Debbie Whitworth, Clink Finance Director

This is easy to make, uses store-bought ingredients and takes less than 30 minutes to put together. It is best made up to 6 hours in advance, so it's perfect for entertaining.

Serves 8

Ingredients

300g packet of Madeira cake
2 tbsp lemon curd
2 tbsp limoncello liqueur
300g frozen raspberries,
   defrosted
250g mascarpone cheese
500g ready-made custard
300ml whipping cream
2 tbsp chopped pistachios

Method

Slice the cake into 6, spread each piece with lemon curd and make 3 'sandwiches'. Cut each into quarters, then place in a 2-litre glass bowl. Drizzle with the limoncello. Scatter the raspberries over, reserving a few good ones for decoration.

Gently whisk the mascarpone and custard together until smooth. Spread over the raspberries.

Whip the cream to soft peaks, then spread on top. Scatter with the pistachios and reserved raspberries.

Orange and ginger nut cream log
Helen Solomon, Clink Training Quality Manager

Serves 6

Pour **300ml whipping cream** into a bowl, add **1½ tbsp icing sugar** and a **drop of vanilla extract**. Whip until thick, then divide between 2 bowls with two-thirds in one and one-third in the other. Pour **150ml orange juice** into another bowl, with a **shot of brandy**, if you like.

Take a **250g packet of ginger nuts**. Get a biscuit, dip it in the juice on both sides and spoon on a blob of cream from the smaller bowl. Dip another biscuit in the juice, then place it on top. Place another dollop of cream on that biscuit, then another juiced-up biscuit. When you have a 3-biscuit stack, spoon a blob of cream on to a **serving plate**, then place on the biscuits, on their sides. Repeat to use up the cream in the small bowl. You should have a log of biscuits.

Use the large bowl of cream to cover the log. Sprinkle a **bashed-up Flake bar** all over and put it in the fridge for at least 30–45 minutes. The biscuits will expand to a cakey texture. Serve, or keep in the fridge, completely covered in cling film, for about 2 days.

Chocolate torte

Paul Clarkson, Clink Head Chef Trainer, HMP Brixton

Serves 8

Ingredients

125g amaretti biscuits,
  crushed
450g 75% cocoa solids
  dark chocolate, broken up
125ml liquid glucose
35ml brandy
35ml navy-strength rum
550ml double cream
cocoa powder, to dust

Method

Line a 23cm springform cake tin with silicone paper and tip the crushed amaretti on to the base.

Melt the chocolate in a heatproof bowl over simmering water with the glucose, brandy and rum. Cool to room temperature.

Whip the cream to soft peaks and fold half into the chocolate mix, then fold the chocolate mixture into the other half of the cream. Pour on to the amaretti crumbs and smooth the top.

Chill for 4 hours in the fridge. Turn the torte upside down on to a plate and remove the tin and paper. (The biscuit crumbs should be facing up.) Sprinkle with cocoa powder and serve.

Mini banoffee tartlets
Caterina Crisci, Clink Friend

Makes about 36

Ingredients
400g jar of salted caramel sauce
2 small bananas, sliced
2 packs of 18 all-butter mini tartlet cases
250g mascarpone cheese
2 tbsp milk
75g milk chocolate, grated

Method
Put the caramel sauce in a microwaveable dish. Microwave, in 10 second bursts, until melted.

Place a slice of banana in the bottom of each pastry case and push it down. Pour a little caramel sauce into the cases, covering the banana, but not reaching to the top of the cases.

Mix the mascarpone in a bowl with the milk to loosen it. Spoon into the cases, filling to the brim (some of the caramel sauce may spill out, and that's fine). Sprinkle grated chocolate on top.

Chill for 1 hour 30 minutes, then serve.

Warm honey-glazed bananas
Tim Wates, Clink Trustee

Serves 5

Ingredients
5 bananas
50g unsalted butter
100g clear honey

Method
Cut the bananas in half lengthways.

Melt the butter in a non-stick frying pan over a medium heat and gently fry the bananas, turning to colour on all sides.

Place the bananas in a serving dish and drizzle the honey over.

Knickerbocker glory
Christopher Moore, Clink Chief Executive

Makes 4 tall sundae glasses

Ingredients
strawberry or raspberry syrup
400g can of fruit salad
500ml tub of vanilla ice cream
300ml whipping cream,
   whipped to soft peaks
chocolate syrup
25g chopped nuts

Method
Squeeze a generous dollop of strawberry or raspberry syrup into 4 tall sundae glasses. Add a spoon of fruit salad, then a scoop of ice cream and push down. Add 2 spoons of cream.

Repeat until the glasses are full.

Top with cream and squeeze the chocolate sauce over. Sprinkle with the nuts and serve with long spoons.

Banana split
Kallum Frances, aged 7, Clink Friend

Makes 1

Ingredients
3 scoops of vanilla ice cream
1 banana
squirty cream
chocolate syrup
strawberry syrup

Method
Put the ice cream balls into a banana-sized dessert dish if you have it, or a small bowl.

Peel the banana, halve it lengthways and place 1 half on either side of the ice cream. Squirt the cream over the bananas.

Decorate the cream with the chocolate and strawberry syrups. Add sprinkles, if you like.

Fruit kebabs   Rosie Davidson, Clink Trustee

Take any **seasonal fruits**, 3–4 varieties, cut so they are of similar size and shape. Push the fruit on to **wooden skewers**, alternating the fruits until the skewers are covered apart from enough room at one end to allow you to pick it up. Serve as it is; this is a good way to encourage children to eat fresh fruit, especially if you add **chocolate sauce** for dipping!

Edwina's chocolate biscuit cake
Lady Edwina Grosvenor, Clink Founder Trustee

Serves 8

Ingredients

120g unsalted butter, softened,
  plus more for the tin
225g Rich Tea biscuits
120g caster sugar
120g good-quality
  dark chocolate, broken up
1 egg, lightly beaten
dark rum (optional)

To decorate
225g dark chocolate
25g white chocolate

Method

Line the base of a 20cm springform cake tin or loaf tin with silicone paper and butter the sides. Break the biscuits into 1–3cm-sized pieces.

Cream the sugar and butter in a bowl. Melt the dark chocolate in a heatproof bowl over simmering water and mix into the butter mixture, then mix in the egg. Add the biscuits and coat well; for an extra zip, add a tot of dark rum.

Place the mixture into the prepared tin, making sure the bottom is well covered as this will be the top of the cake when it is served. Set in the fridge for 3 hours. Remove from the fridge and allow to slightly lose its chill. Separately melt the dark and white chocolate for decoration. Flip the cake out of the tin and cover with dark chocolate, then drizzle with white chocolate. Leave to set before serving.

Tear-and-share chocolate spread pastry
Vanessa Frances, Clink Fundraiser

Buy **2 × 320g packets of ready-rolled puff pastry**. Preheat the oven according to the pastry packet instructions. **Flour** a work surface and roll both sheets of pastry into longer rectangles. Spread 1 rectangle generously with **chocolate-hazelnut spread** and place the other rectangle on top. Now you have a choice. You can twist the layers and place into a **loaf tin**, as in the photo; or place on a **baking tray**, lightly cut into the top layer, making shapes, letters or a message and at the same time revealing the chocolate below; or fold back strips of the top layer, twist and seal on top.

Bake in the oven according to the pastry packet instructions. Serve warm, to a hungry crowd.

Chocolate bombe

Jane Sanderson, Clink Director of Operations and Training

Serves 8

Lightly whip **450ml double cream** with **30g caster sugar**. Spoon into a freezable **1.7-litre pudding basin**. Using the back of a large spoon, spread the cream evenly to line the inside of the basin, leaving a large hollow in the centre. Cover and put in the freezer to set firm.

Break **175g dark chocolate** into a heatproof bowl and set over a saucepan of simmering water (make sure the bowl does not touch the water). Add **30g unsalted butter**. Meanwhile, separate **6 eggs**. Whisk the egg whites until stiff. Remove the melted chocolate and butter mixture from the heat and beat in the egg yolks, then fold in the egg whites. Pour into the hollow inside the cream-lined basin, cover and replace in the freezer overnight.

About 2 hours before serving, unmould by dipping the bowl in cold water and easing out with a palette knife. Leave in the fridge to soften for 2 hours. Cover with **chocolate curls** to serve.

Christmas stollen-misu

Daniel Ayton, Clink Chef Ambassador

Serves 6

Ingredients

500g shop-bought stollen
80ml dark rum
200ml cold espresso coffee
finely grated zest of 1 unwaxed
    orange and juice of ½
30ml honey
500g cream cheese
400ml double cream
6 tbsp golden caster sugar
2g ground cinnamon
festive sprinkles (optional)

Method

Chop the stollen into 1cm cubes and place half in a serving bowl, or individual glasses. Mix the rum with the coffee and put half the mixture into the bowl or glasses with the stollen.

Mix together half the orange zest, the orange juice, honey and cream cheese. Whip the cream with 5 tbsp of the sugar. Fold into the cream cheese mixture. Layer half the cream cheese over the stollen; then add the remaining stollen. Drizzle with the remaining rum mixture and top with the remaining cream cheese. Chill for 30 minutes.

Mix the last 1 tbsp of sugar, the cinnamon and the last of the zest, and use this to decorate, with the sprinkles (if using).

Muscovado heaven
Prue Leith, CBE, DL, Clink Chef Ambassador

This is the simplest catering trick that I once did for a party of gourmets, chefs and food writers… and hugely enjoyed hearing them discussing the ingredients. 'Must be that new mascarpone from Northern Italy.' 'No, no, it's Devon cream posset with a damson glaze,' and so on. Meanwhile, it's just cream, yogurt and sugar. And it takes 2 minutes, max, to make.

Serves as many as you want

Put some **fruit compote, jam, fruit** or what have you in a **shallow dish** or **individual cocktail glasses**. Stir **equal parts double cream and plain yogurt** together until gloopy-thick but not set. Pour over the fruit.

Sprinkle really heavily with **dark muscovado sugar** (no other sugar will do!) and put in the fridge for 30 minutes or so. The sugar will dissolve into a dark lake. If you like a bit of crunch, sprinkle a little more sugar on top before serving, or serve with a thin sweet biscuit.

Easy Eton mess
Kevin McGrath OBE, DL, Clink Founder Trustee

Serves 6

Ingredients
200g cream cheese

50g icing sugar

2 drops of vanilla extract

3 tbsp single cream

12 large strawberries

6 ready-made meringue nests

6 small mint leaves

Method
Put the cream cheese into a bowl, add the sugar, vanilla extract and the cream and mix together.

Slice each strawberry in half.

Spoon the cream mixture into the meringue nests. Arrange 4 pieces of strawberry sticking out in each nest and place a mint leaf in the middle of each to serve.

Fruit

Blueberry pancakes with maple syrup

Ingredients

200g self-raising flour
1 tsp baking powder
pinch of salt
1 egg, lightly beaten
10g unsalted butter, melted
300ml whole milk
150g blueberries
sunflower oil, to cook
50ml maple syrup
100g crème fraîche

Method

Beat together the flour, baking powder, salt, beaten egg, melted butter and milk, then stir in half the blueberries.

Place a non-stick frying pan over a medium-high heat, and add a splash of oil. Ladle in the batter, using 1–2 tbsp for each pancake and being careful not to overcrowd the pan. Cook the pancakes until they look dry on top, then flip them and cook until golden on the other side, too. Remove from the pan and keep warm while you make the remaining pancakes in the same way.

Serve the pancakes drizzled with the maple syrup, sprinkling over the remaining blueberries and serving the crème fraîche alongside.

Welsh summer griddle cakes
Eleri Retallick, Clink Friend

Makes 24

Ingredients

300g plain flour
4 tsp baking powder
3½ tbsp caster sugar, plus more
   to serve (optional)
2 eggs, separated
50g unsalted butter, melted
300ml whole milk
2 strawberries, chopped,
   plus more to serve (optional)
flavourless oil
lightly whipped cream, to serve

Method

Sift the flour and baking powder into a bowl and stir in the sugar, egg yolks, butter and milk until smooth. In a separate bowl, whisk the egg whites until fairly stiff, then fold into the mixture. Add the chopped strawberries.

Lightly oil a frying pan, then place over a medium heat. Pour in tablespoons of mixture, cook for 2 minutes, flip and cook for 2 minutes. Remove from the pan and sprinkle with sugar.

Repeat to cook all the mixture. Serve with a sprinkle of sugar and strawberries, if you like, and cream on the side.

Lemon posset, Daniel Ayton, Clink Chef Ambassador

Ingredients

850ml double cream
250g caster sugar
finely grated zest and
  juice of 3 unwaxed lemons
edible flowers, to serve
  (optional)
whipped cream, to serve
  (optional)

Method

Boil the cream and sugar for 2–3 minutes, add the lemon zest and juice, mix well and leave to cool slightly.

Pour into glasses, cover and leave to set in the fridge. To serve, add edible flowers and pipe on whipped cream, if you like. Or just serve with biscuits.

Shortbread and lemon tartlets
Paul Clarkson, Clink Head Chef Trainer, HMP Brixton

Makes 4

Ingredients

For the shortbread

125g unsalted butter, softened
1 vanilla pod
55g caster sugar
180g plain flour

For the filling

600ml double cream
200g caster sugar
finely grated zest of
  3 unwaxed lemons,
  plus 75ml lemon juice,
  plus lemon zest to serve

Method

To make the bases, put the butter in a bowl, then split the vanilla pod lengthways and scrape in the seeds. Add the sugar and beat until smooth. Beat in the flour until it all comes together, then wrap in cling film and chill for 20 minutes.

Preheat the oven to 190°C/fan 170°C/375°F/gas 5.

Once rested, roll the shortbread out to 5mm thick and use it to line 10cm tartlet tins, leaving a little extra pastry hanging over the edge for shrinkage. Place baking parchment on each, fill with baking beans (see page 83) and bake for 15–20 minutes until light golden. Chill, then trim off excess pastry with a knife.

To make the filling, simmer the cream and sugar together for 90 seconds, stirring continually. Remove from the heat. Add the lemon zest and juice. Pour into the shortbread bases and chill for 2–3 hours. Serve topped with a pinch of lemon zest.

Tarte Tatin with rosemary and almonds
Daniel Galmiche, Clink Chef Ambassador

When you open the oven door, you will be enveloped in the incredible perfume of rosemary-scented apples.

Serves 8

Ingredients

220g ready-made all-butter puff pastry
plain flour, to dust
120g caster sugar
40g unsalted butter
1 rosemary sprig, leaves picked and roughly chopped, plus 1 whole sprig to serve (optional)
4–5 apples, such as Cox's, peeled, halved and cored
large pinch of toasted flaked almonds, plus more to serve
crème fraîche, to serve

Method

Roll out the pastry on a lightly floured surface, then cut out a circle slightly bigger than a 20cm flameproof cake or tart tin. Roll the pastry over the rolling pin and unroll on a baking sheet, cover with cling film and chill for 30 minutes to prevent it from shrinking while cooking.

Preheat the oven to 190°C/fan 170°C/375°F/gas 5.

Melt the sugar gently in the cake tin over a medium heat until golden brown, then remove from the heat and stir in the butter. Sprinkle one-quarter of the rosemary over, adding the whole sprig of rosemary now, if using. Arrange the apples tightly around the edge of the tin, then make smaller circles to fill the tin. Sprinkle with the almonds and remaining rosemary, then place the pastry on top, pushing the edges down over the apples. Bake for 20 minutes until the pastry is golden brown and crisp.

Remove and leave to cool for a few minutes. Put an upside-down serving plate on top, then flip the tart out of the tin and sprinkle with more almonds. Eat warm, with crème fraîche.

Normandy tart
Prue Leith, CBE, DL, Clink Chef Ambassador

Serves 8

Ingredients

For the pastry

225g plain flour
150g unsalted butter,
    chopped
1 egg
pinch of salt
60g caster sugar

For the filling

175g unsalted butter,
    softened
175g caster sugar
225g ground almonds
2 eggs
1 tbsp calvados, kirsch,
    or whatever you like
a few drops of almond
    extract

For the topping

3–5 eating apples,
    depending on size
½ jar (about 160g)
    of smooth apricot jam

Method

For the pastry, whizz everything together in a food processor until the mix forms a ball. Roll out between 2 sheets of cling film until big enough to line a 25cm tart tin. Line the tin. Chill for 30 minutes.

Preheat the oven to 200°C/fan 180°C/400°F/gas 6 and put a metal tray inside to heat. If the dish is porcelain, bake the pastry case blind (see page 83). If it's metal, don't bother.

Whizz everything for the filling in the food processor (no need to wash the bowl after the pastry), then spread it in the lined tin. Peel the apples if you like, but don't feel you have to. Core them and cut in half from stalk to flower end. Slice each half-apple finely, keeping the slices in order. Arrange them on the filling.

Set the flan in the middle of the hot oven, on the hot baking tray, and bake for 15 minutes. Meanwhile, gently melt the jam in a small saucepan with 1 tbsp water. Paint the apples with some hot jam.

Reduce the oven temperature to 180°C/fan 160°C/350°F/ gas 4. Bake for 30 minutes, until the filling is firm and brown.

Remove the tart from the oven and give it another brush with the jam if you think it needs it.

This tart is best eaten warm or at room temperature. Do not chill it, or the pastry will soften. If you make it in advance, freeze it and then reheat for 20 minutes at 180°C/fan 160°C/350°F/gas 4 and leave to cool; this will crisp up the pastry once more.

Traditional apple charlotte
Derek Casey, Clink General Manager Trainer, HMP Brixton

Serves 4

Ingredients

450g apples, half Bramley,
    half Cox's, if possible
30g caster sugar
110g unsalted butter, melted
8 slices of white bread,
    crusts removed

Method

Peel, core and thinly slice the apples, put in a saucepan with the sugar and 25g of the butter, then cook over a low heat until soft. Leave to cool. Gently melt the remaining butter, brush it on the bread, cut the bread into rectangles and use most of it to line a 600ml pudding basin, or 4 individual pudding basins, leaving no gaps. Pour the cold apple mixture into the basin(s), cover with overlapping bread slices to seal, then place an ovenproof plate and weight on top for 1 hour.

When you are ready to cook, preheat the oven to 200°C/fan 180°C/400°F/gas 6. Bake with the weight on top for 35 minutes. Remove the plate and weight and bake for 10 minutes more to crisp the top. Let it settle for a minute, then turn out to serve. Great with custard (see page 59).

Double apple and frangipane tart
Matt Tebbutt, Clink Chef Ambassador

Serves 10

Make a frangipane: beat **250g each softened unsalted butter and caster sugar** until pale. Beat in **250g ground almonds**, then **4 eggs**, one at a time. Chill.

Peel, core and chop **2 Bramley apples** and put in a saucepan with **1 split vanilla pod** and a little water. Place over a low heat until the apples disintegrate. Add caster sugar to taste. Leave to cool. Meanwhile, soak a **big handful of raisins** in enough **warm white port** to cover.

Preheat the oven to 150°C/fan 130°C/300°F/gas 2. Spoon the apple purée over a **30cm raw sweet pastry case**, then peel, core and halve **6 Cox's apples**. Scatter the drained raisins over the apple purée, then add the halved apples. Pipe the frangipane around. Bake for 40–50 minutes until golden; an inserted knife should come out clean. Serve warm with crème fraîche.

Pinot Grigio poached peaches

This recipe looks and tastes especially striking with white peaches, if you can get them, though yellow peaches work beautifully, too.

Serves 4

Ingredients

1 large unwaxed orange
4 large white-fleshed peaches, if you can get them, otherwise any peach will do
375ml Pinot Grigio (or any white wine, as long as it is not too sweet)
175g caster sugar
a few nibbed pistachios (optional)

Method

With a vegetable peeler, remove the zest from the orange, being careful not to remove the white pith as well. With a sharp knife, cut the zest into fine matchstick-like strips. Juice the orange.

Peel, halve and pit the peaches and place in a large heatproof bowl.

Put the wine in a saucepan and bring to the boil, then add the sugar, orange zest and orange juice and stir until the sugar is dissolved. Simmer until the liquid reduces by half and becomes syrupy. Pour the whole lot over the peaches and cover with a lid or cling film. Leave to cool.

Vibrant berry terrine

Mark Sillery, Clink Director of Support Work and Mentoring

Serves 10

Ingredients

350g small strawberries
225g raspberries
350g blackcurrants, redcurrants and blueberries, or preferred seasonal berries
1 vanilla pod
425ml sparkling rosé wine, prosecco, fruit juice, or elderflower drink
50g caster sugar
2 x 12g sachets of powdered gelatine
1 tbsp lemon juice
mint or basil leaves, to taste

Method

Line a 900g non-stick loaf tin with cling film all around, covering the base and sides. Halve any large strawberries and remove the stalks from all the berries. Gently mix the fruits together.

Split the vanilla pod and scrape out the seeds, keeping the pod and seeds separate. In a small saucepan, heat half the wine, juice or drink until it is about to simmer, then whisk in the sugar, gelatine, vanilla seeds and pod. Make sure that everything has dissolved completely before adding the remaining wine, juice or drink and the lemon juice. Pour the liquid into a jug and leave to cool. Meanwhile, rip or shred the herb leaves and add to the berry mix.

Layer the mixed fruit in the tin (arrange the bottom layer carefully, as this will be on top when the terrine is turned out). You can arrange in layers, or mixed, whatever suits. Both look great.

Remove the vanilla pod from the cooled liquid and gently pour all but 150ml over the fruit. Lay a sheet of cling film over, carefully place another loaf tin – or a piece of thick card, cut to size – on top and add 2 cans of tomatoes or similar weights. Refrigerate for about 1 hour, or until set. Warm up the remaining 150ml liquid, remove the weights and cling film, and pour the liquid over the terrine. Re-cover with cling film and return to the fridge overnight to set firm.

Dip the tin quickly in hot water, or heat with a blowtorch, then invert on to a plate. Slice using a hot, sharp knife. Serve with cream, ice cream or crème fraîche flavoured with orange zest.

Vegan blueberry muffins
Debbie Whitworth, Clink Finance Director

Makes 6

Ingredients

180g plain flour
110g caster sugar
½ tsp salt
2 tsp baking powder
1 large, very ripe banana
100ml vegetable oil
150ml non-dairy milk
150g fresh or frozen
   blueberries

Method

Preheat the oven to 220°C/fan 200°C/425°F/gas 7.

Measure all the dry ingredients into a bowl. Mash the banana in a separate bowl until smooth, then add the oil and milk and mix until combined (it may take a minute or so). Add the blueberries and then mix all that into the dry ingredients.

Fill muffin cases two-thirds full and bake for 16–20 minutes or until a knife comes out clean.

Banana tart
Shaila Ramasur, Clink Friend

Serves 6

Ingredients

250g plain flour, plus more
   to dust
175g unsalted butter,
   chilled and chopped
10 ripe bananas
4 tbsp light brown sugar
1 tbsp vanilla extract
1 egg
1 tbsp milk

Method

Mix the flour and butter in a food processor until it resembles breadcrumbs. Add 1 tbsp water to bring it together, then chill for 1 hour. Mash the bananas and sugar in a pan. Cook over a low heat, stirring until thick. Stir in the vanilla and leave to cool.

Preheat the oven to 150°C/fan 130°C/300°F/gas 2. Roll out half the pastry on a floured surface and use it to line a 20cm tart tin. Roll out the rest and cut into 1cm-thick strips. Spoon the filling into the case. Mix the egg and milk and brush the pastry rim. Arrange the strips over in a lattice, sealing against the rim. Brush with egg. Bake for 15 minutes until golden.

Making berry coulis

STEP ONE
Place berries into a food processor (remove any stalks first) and whizz briefly to break them up.

STEP TWO
Add a little icing sugar, then whizz again.

STEP THREE
Taste the fruit purée: depending on the sweetness or tartness of the berries, you may need to add more icing sugar to sweeten, or lemon juice to sharpen.

STEP FOUR
Pour the fruit purée into a sieve placed over a bowl.

STEP FIVE
Push through the sieve with a spoon, to produce a smooth, seed-free coulis.

Raspberry cheesecake brownies

Helen Solomon, Clink Training Quality Manager

This decadent chocolate brownie recipe can also be served as a pudding. If you prefer, omit the raspberries and add a drained 400g can of cherries, each fruit halved, instead.

Makes 16

Ingredients

For the brownie

175g unsalted butter, chopped, plus more for the tin

125g 70% cocoa solids dark chocolate, chopped

300g caster sugar

pinch of salt

3 eggs

100g plain flour

300g raspberries

For the cheesecake

200g low-fat cream cheese

50g caster sugar

1 egg

seeds from 1 vanilla pod, or 1 tsp vanilla bean paste

Method

Preheat the oven to 180°C/fan 160°C/350°F/gas 4. Lightly butter a 20.5cm square tin and line with baking parchment. Whisk together all the ingredients for the cheesecake until smooth.

For the brownie, melt the chocolate and butter in a pan over a low heat, stirring occasionally. Take it off the heat and stir in the sugar and salt. Mix in the eggs, one at a time, then the flour, until well combined. Stir in the raspberries. Scrape into the prepared tin and level off. Dollop on spoonfuls of the cheesecake layer, then run a skewer through the mix for a marbled effect.

Bake for 35–40 minutes, or until firm. Cool completely in the tin, then chill for at least 2 hours to set. Serve in squares, either chilled or at room temperature.

Almond-orange cake
Helen Ash, Clink HR Consultant

This moist cake makes a great dessert with segmented oranges and crème fraîche.

Serves 6

Ingredients

2 thin-skinned oranges
a little oil, for the tin
135g caster sugar
4 eggs, separated
165g ground almonds
1 tbsp orange blossom water

Method

Put the oranges in a pan, just-cover with water, bring to the boil and simmer for 1 hour. Halve, discard pips, then whizz to purée. Oil a 23cm springform tin; line with baking parchment. Preheat the oven to 180°C/fan 160°C/350°F/gas 4.

Whisk three-quarters of the sugar and the egg yolks in a food processor until thick and creamy. Add the almonds, orange purée and orange blossom water. Mix well. Whisk the egg whites until stiff, whisking in the remaining sugar, then fold into the batter. Scrape into the tin and bake for 50–60 minutes. It should be golden and a skewer should come out clean.

Spiced blackberry and plum crumble
Simon McKinnon-Brahams, Chef Trainer, HMP Brixton

Serves 8

Preheat the oven to 200°C/fan 180°C/400°F/gas 6. Put **140g each plain flour and chopped cold unsalted butter** into a food processor with **85g soft brown sugar** and **1 tsp ground cinnamon**. Blitz to a crumble texture.

Put **1kg halved and pitted plums** in a large saucepan with **2 star anise**, **1 cinnamon stick**, **1 vanilla pod**, split lengthways, and the **juice of ½ lemon**. Add **1 tbsp soft brown sugar** and **350g blackberries**. Cook over a low heat for around 20 minutes until the plums are soft. Remove the spices, place into an **oven dish** and top with the crumble. Bake for 20 minutes until golden. Leave to stand for 10 minutes, then serve with cream or ice cream.

Raspberry and tequila nieve
Thomasina Miers, Clink Chef Ambassador

A simple water ice, hugely popular in Mexico thanks to the heat and the enormous range of fruits. Easy to make ahead, this makes a refreshing end to a summer dinner.

Serves 4

Ingredients
200g caster sugar
500g raspberries
juice of ½ lime
3 tbsp tequila

Method
Gently heat 150g of the sugar with 150ml water; when the sugar dissolves, boil for 3 minutes. Purée the raspberries and remaining sugar in a food processor. Pass through a sieve to remove the pips. Add the syrup, lime juice and 1 tbsp of the tequila (too much alcohol means it won't freeze).

Pour into a shallow freezable dish, then freeze for 2 hours until part-frozen. Mix with a fork to break up the ice. Freeze for another hour. Repeat until you have a crunchy frozen nieve. Serve with the extra tequila poured on top.

Finlay's boozy summer pudding jelly
Finlay Scott, Clink Chairman and Founder Trustee

Serves 8

Ingredients

175g packet of sponge fingers
3 punnets of strawberries
2 punnets of raspberries
2 punnets of blackcurrants
4 leaves of gelatine
150ml elderflower cordial
2 heaped tbsp caster sugar
400ml prosecco, chilled

Method

Line a pudding mould with cling film, then line it with sponge fingers, cutting them up first, if needed, to cover the base. Mix the fruit, tumble it into the middle and refrigerate.

Put the gelatine into a heatproof bowl with a little cold water to soak, then squeeze it to remove excess water, pour away the water, and return the gelatine to the now-empty bowl with the cordial. Set the bowl over a saucepan of simmering water; it should not touch the water. Place over a medium heat and stir constantly until the gelatine and cordial become a syrup. Add the sugar, stir until dissolved, then remove the bowl from the heat and let it sit at room temperature for a minute.

Take the mould and prosecco out of the fridge. Pour the prosecco into the cordial mix, then pour this over the fruit. Some of the fruit might rise to the top; just push it back down into the jelly mix so that it is sealed and will then keep well in the fridge (keep doing this over the next few hours as the jelly sets). Put back into the fridge to set.

To serve, dip the mould into a bowl of hot water to loosen the outside of the jelly, then turn it out on to a plate.

Edwina's rhubarb crumble and custard

Lady Edwina Grosvenor, Clink Founder Trustee

Serves 4

Ingredients

For the crumble

250g cold unsalted butter,
   cut into small chunks
400g plain flour
200g golden caster sugar
pinch of salt

For the filling

700g rhubarb, trimmed and
   chopped into 2.5cm pieces
a little unsalted butter
2 tbsp golden caster sugar,
   plus more to sprinkle
juice of ½ lemon

For the custard

500ml whole milk
8 egg yolks
140g vanilla sugar
3 tbsp cornflour
3 tbsp plain flour

Method

Preheat the oven to 180°C/fan 160°C/350°F/gas 4.

Place all the ingredients for the crumble mixture in a large bowl. Rub the butter into the flour, sugar and salt, lifting and dropping the mixture lightly through your fingers.

Put the rhubarb into a buttered ovenproof dish. Sprinkle with the sugar, pour over the lemon juice and dot small pieces of butter over. Cover the fruit with the crumble mixture, sprinkling over a little extra sugar. Bake for 35–40 minutes, or until golden brown.

Meanwhile, make the custard. Heat the milk in a heavy-based saucepan until it comes just to the boil, then take off the heat immediately. In a bowl, beat together the egg yolks, vanilla sugar and flours. Pour the milk slowly over the egg mixture, beating well. Return the mixture to the saucepan and place over a low heat, stirring, for 8–10 minutes, until the mixture begins to thicken. Remove from the heat and serve with the crumble.

Red wine figs, mascarpone and lavender

Serves 4

Ingredients

200ml red wine
8 ripe strawberries, roughly chopped
100g granulated sugar
8 figs, ideally black figs, not too ripe, halved lengthways
175g mascarpone cheese
25g icing sugar
lavender flowers, to serve
pistachios, chopped, to serve

Method

Put the wine, strawberries and sugar into a large frying pan. Bring to the boil and simmer for 5 minutes; take care not to allow the pan to boil dry, as you will need the liquid for the sauce, so add water if necessary.

Remove from the heat and place the figs in the hot liquid, turning the fruits and spooning over the hot syrup for 2 minutes. Leave the figs to cool in the syrup.

Put the mascarpone and icing sugar into a bowl and beat well. Remove the figs from the syrup, then put the wine and strawberry syrup in a food processor and blend until smooth.

Arrange the figs on 4 dessert plates with the mascarpone, then spoon some syrup over. Decorate with lavender flowers, scatter with pistachios and serve.

Dairy

Zabaglione

Ingredients
8 egg yolks
100g caster sugar
25ml Marsala or sherry

Method
Put a heatproof bowl over a pan of just-simmering water and place the egg yolks and sugar into it. Make sure the base of the bowl does not touch the water.

Using an electric whisk, start whisking the egg yolks and sugar in the bowl over the water. The mixture will become pale and thick like whipped cream, and it should triple in volume and become very frothy. This takes up to 15 minutes. Continue whisking while you slowly pour in the Marsala or sherry.

Pour into 8 dessert glasses and serve immediately.

Cati's leche frita
Caterina Crisci, Clink Friend

Leche frita ('fried milk') is a traditional Spanish dessert recipe.

Serves 4

Ingredients
60g plain flour, plus more
  to coat
60g cornflour
115g caster sugar,
  plus more to serve
950ml whole milk
1 cinnamon stick, plus
  ground cinnamon to serve
1 tbsp sunflower oil
2 eggs, lightly beaten
175ml olive oil

Method
Mix the flour, cornflour and sugar into 250ml of the milk. Put the rest of the milk and the cinnamon stick into a saucepan, then boil for 10 minutes. Strain through a sieve, then add it to the paste. Return this to a clean saucepan. Simmer over a low heat, stirring, for 10 minutes. Oil a baking tray with sunflower oil, then pour the mixture on to the tray. Leave until cold.

Cut into 10 × 5cm rectangles. Set up 2 dishes, filling 1 with flour, and the second with eggs. Gently, coat each milk rectangle with flour, then with egg. Heat the olive oil in a large frying pan. Fry the pieces in batches, turning once, until golden. Remove with a slotted spoon and drain on kitchen paper. Keep warm while you fry the rest. Sprinkle with sugar and ground cinnamon and serve hot.

Rose and yogurt jelly, pomegranate gel
Daniel Ayton, Clink Chef Ambassador

Serves 6

Ingredients

For the pomegranate gel

1.5g agar agar

250ml fresh pomegranate juice

For the yogurt jelly

300ml double cream

75ml whole milk

40g caster sugar

2 leaves of gelatine,
    soaked in cold water

300ml full-fat yogurt

rose water, to taste

unsalted pistachios, to serve

pomegranate seeds, to serve

Method

Stir the agar agar into the pomegranate juice in a saucepan, bring the juice to the boil and simmer for 1 minute. Pour into a lined baking tray and leave at room temperature. Do not move the gel until completely set, as movement will disturb the agar and prevent it from setting. Once set, cut into small cubes.

Bring the cream, milk and sugar to the boil in a saucepan, simmer for a minute, then remove from the heat. Drain the soaked gelatine, squeeze to remove excess water and stir into the hot cream. Stir in the yogurt and add rose water to taste.

Pass through a fine sieve and pour it into 6 dariole moulds, or use glasses, about 140ml in volume. Refrigerate to set. Serve with the gel cubes, pistachios and pomegranate seeds.

Chestnut soufflé, Prue Leith, Clink Chef Ambassador

Serves 6

Ingredients

unsalted butter, for the dish

4 eggs, separated

400g sweetened chestnut
    purée

4 tbsp brandy

whipped cream, mascarpone
    or Greek yogurt, to serve

Method

Preheat the oven to 180°C/fan 160°C/350°F/gas 4. Lightly butter a 1.5-litre soufflé dish. Whisk the yolks until pale and thick. In a separate bowl, whisk the chestnut purée and brandy until pale coffee-coloured. Mix both together. Whisk the whites until stiff, then fold them in. Tip into the dish and bake for 35–40 minutes. (To tell if it is done, give the dish a shove. If it wobbles all over, it needs 10 minutes. If it wobbles in the middle it has a nice runny centre. If it doesn't wobble it's cooked through, but you'll definitely need cream, or a sauce.) Serve with cream, mascarpone or Greek yogurt. Have fun.

Rose water ice cream

Ingredients

275ml whole milk
4 large egg yolks
110g caster sugar
280ml double cream
3 tbsp rose water

Method

Heat the milk slowly in a heavy-based saucepan to boiling point. Meanwhile, whisk the egg yolks and sugar together until smooth. Pour the hot milk over them, whisking all the time. Return the mixture to the saucepan and cook over a low heat, but do not allow to boil, stirring constantly, until it thickens and coats the back of the spoon. Pour into a bowl, cool, then chill. Stir in the cream and rose water, then either churn in an ice-cream maker, or pour into a shallow plastic container and put in the freezer until frozen solid (after 2 hours of freezing, whisk it to remove any ice crystals at the edges; repeat twice more during freezing).

Easy salted caramel ice cream
Alexandra Bertram, Clink PR and Marketing

Serves 8

Ingredients

340g caster sugar
1 tbsp golden syrup
1 tbsp black treacle
450ml double cream
300ml semi-skimmed milk
2 tsp sea salt flakes
8 egg yolks

Method

Heat a heavy-based saucepan over a medium heat. Once hot, tip in 280g of the caster sugar. Heat, moving the pan occasionally, until the sugar melts to a nice caramel colour. Add the syrup, treacle and cream and bring to a gentle boil, stirring. Add the milk and a generous pinch of salt and stir again. Leaving that to gently return to the boil, beat the egg yolks in a large heatproof bowl with the remaining sugar until pale and mousse-like. Slowly pour in the hot caramel, whisking. Pass it through a sieve into a freezable container and chill. Once chilled, sprinkle most of the remaining salt on top and place in the freezer.

Set a timer for 20 minutes at a time, stirring the ice cream well with a spatula each time. After 2 hours, sprinkle the last of the salt on top. Leave to fully set for at least 4 hours before serving. It will be a soft ice cream.

Buttermilk puddings with blackberries
Michael Hendry, The Bell at Shenington, Oxfordshire

Makes 6

Ingredients

400ml double cream
1 vanilla pod
3 leaves of gelatine
250g caster sugar, plus 1 tbsp
finely grated zest and juice of 1 unwaxed lemon
600ml buttermilk
large punnet of blackberries
100ml Chambord (black raspberry liqueur), or other berry liqueur

Method

Pour the cream into a bowl. Split the vanilla pod and scrape the seeds into the cream. Put the gelatine into a separate small bowl and just-cover with cold water. Leave for 5 minutes.

Measure 200ml of the vanilla cream into another bowl and whip to soft peaks. Put the remainder in a saucepan with the 250g of sugar, the vanilla pod and lemon zest and bring to the boil. Remove from the heat and stir in the lemon juice. Squeeze the excess water from the gelatine and stir the gelatine in, too. Strain into a jug.

Put the buttermilk in a bowl, then gradually whisk in the hot cream. Leave to cool. When cold, fold in the whipped cream. Spoon the mixture into moulds or glasses and refrigerate overnight.

Put the blackberries in a bowl. Warm the 1 tbsp of sugar and the Chambord in a saucepan, then pour over the fruit, gently mixing to macerate the berries. Serve with the puddings.

Pannacotta with beetroot and lime syrup

Makes 6

Ingredients

2 leaves of gelatine
600ml double cream
160g caster sugar
2 tbsp dark rum
1 vanilla pod, split and
    seeds scraped out
finely grated zest and juice of
    2 unwaxed limes,
    plus lime zest to serve
1 raw beetroot, peeled
    and finely chopped

Method

Put the gelatine leaves in a small bowl, cover with cold water and leave to soak until soft. Heat the cream with 60g of the sugar, the rum and vanilla seeds; bring to the boil, then boil for a few seconds. Let cool a little, then squeeze out the gelatine and mix in to dissolve. Pour into 6 teacups and chill overnight.

Put the remaining 100g of sugar in a heavy-based saucepan with the lime zest and juice. When the sugar is clear, the syrup is ready. Spoon in the beetroot and leave to cool.

Leave the pannacotta at room temperature for 1 hour, then spoon on the syrup and lime zest to serve.

Pannacotta from the Aosta valley
Antonio Carluccio OBE, Clink Chef Ambassador

Makes 8

Ingredients

750ml single cream
200ml whole milk
250g caster sugar
seeds from 1 vanilla pod
½ tsp vanilla extract
2 tbsp peach liqueur,
    or dark rum
3 leaves of gelatine
strips of candied orange peel

Method

Put everything except the gelatine and candied peel into a saucepan and very slowly bring to the boil.

Soften the gelatine in a little water. Lift out, squeeze out the excess water and add to the hot cream mixture just before it comes to the boil. Stir until the gelatine has dissolved, then pour into 8 ramekins or dariole moulds.

Leave to cool, then refrigerate until set. To unmould, dip the base of each mould into warm water for a few seconds, then turn out on to small serving plates.

To serve, decorate with small pieces of candied orange peel.

Tiramisu

Antonio Carluccio OBE, Clink Chef Ambassador

Makes 4

Ingredients

2 egg yolks
100g caster sugar
½ tsp vanilla extract
400g mascarpone cheese
80ml single cream
milk, if needed
400ml strong espresso coffee
4 tbsp Kahlua or Tia Maria
18 Savoyard biscuits
cocoa powder, to dust

Method

In a small bowl, beat the egg yolks, 80g of the caster sugar and the vanilla together. In a second larger bowl, mix the mascarpone with the cream. Mix both together; should the mixture be too dense, add a few drops of milk.

Mix the coffee, liqueur and remaining 20g of caster sugar in a third bowl. Dip the biscuits briefly into the mixture (don't let them absorb too much) and use to line 4 ramekins.

Put in a layer of the mascarpone mixture, then top with more biscuits, finishing with mascarpone, piped in or not, as you prefer. Dust with a little cocoa powder and chill until serving.

Ricotta and orange cake

Serves 10

Ingredients

90g unsalted butter, softened
3 tbsp plain flour, more to dust
40g raisins
finely grated zest and juice of
   1 large unwaxed orange
150g vanilla sugar
2 eggs
1½ tsp baking powder
finely grated zest of
   1 unwaxed lemon
450g ricotta cheese

Method

Preheat the oven to 180°C/fan 160°C/350°F/gas 4. Butter a 25cm cake tin, then dust it with flour, tipping out the excess.

Put the raisins in a saucepan with the orange juice, place over a medium heat, bring to the boil, then reduce to a simmer for just a few minutes until the raisins plump up. Leave to cool.

Cream the butter and sugar and gradually beat in the eggs. Fold in the flour and baking powder, and orange and lemon zests. Drain the ricotta and stir it into the mixture until fully incorporated. Add the raisins and fold them in, too.

Spoon into the prepared tin and bake for 55 minutes.

Cardamom and pistachio rice pudding
Kerry Rickett, Clink Head Chef Trainer, HMP Styal

Serves 4

Ingredients

For the rice pudding

100g pudding rice
400ml whole milk
50g caster sugar
1 vanilla pod
50g pistachio nibs,
   plus more to serve
½ tsp green cardamom
   seeds, ground

For the compote

370g plums (frozen will do),
   halved and pitted
1 tbsp brown sugar

Method

Place the rice, milk and sugar in a non-stick saucepan and mix to combine. Split the vanilla pod lengthways and scrape the seeds into the pan. Place over a medium heat and bring to a simmer, then reduce the heat and cook gently until all the milk has been absorbed. This will take around 30 minutes. Stir in the nuts and cardamom towards the end of the cooking time.

Check the rice is cooked: it should be soft with no bite. If it isn't, add a little more milk and cook for a few more minutes.

Meanwhile, place the plums in a small saucepan over a low heat with the brown sugar and bring to a simmer. Cook for 20–30 minutes until soft, then leave to cool.

Serve the rice pudding with the plums, sprinkling with more pistachio nibs.

Making custard

STEP ONE
Pour 570ml whole milk into a saucepan with 55ml single cream, then scrape in the seeds from 1 vanilla pod. Slowly bring to a simmer.

STEP TWO
Meanwhile, in a bowl, whisk 4 egg yolks with 30g caster sugar and 2 tsp cornflour.

STEP THREE
Pour the hot milk mixture on to the egg mixture, whisking constantly, then return to the pan over a low heat.

STEP FOUR
Gently stir the custard until it thickens enough to coat the back of the spoon: if you draw a finger through it, the channel will stay clear.

Makes about 600ml

Sicilian cheesecake
Caterina Crisci, Clink Friend

Serves 6

Ingredients
40g cold unsalted butter, chopped, plus more for the tin
75g plain flour
60g caster sugar
250g ricotta cheese
2 eggs, separated
50g ground almonds
45g sultanas
35g chopped candied peel
25g toasted pine nuts
finely grated zest of 1 unwaxed lemon
4 tbsp double cream
icing sugar, to dust (optional)
dried orange slices, to serve (optional)

Method
Preheat the oven to 200°C/fan 180°C/400°F/gas 6. Butter an 18cm springform cake tin and line the base with silicone paper.

Rub the butter into the flour with your fingertips, to form a crumble texture. Mix in 10g of the sugar. Tip the mixture into the prepared tin and spread evenly before pressing down with a spoon. Bake for 10 minutes, or until golden in colour. Remove from the oven and reduce the oven temperature to 160°C/fan 140°C/325°F/gas 3.

In a bowl, mix the ricotta, remaining sugar and egg yolks, beating with a wooden spoon until smooth. Stir in the ground almonds, sultanas, candied peel, pine nuts, lemon zest and cream.

Whisk the egg whites in a separate clean bowl until stiff, then carefully fold into the ricotta mixture, taking care not to beat the air out of the egg whites. Pour the mixture into the cake tin over the crumble base and bake for 45–50 minutes, or until it sets and is golden in colour.

Leave to cool, then remove from the tin and place on a serving plate, dusting with icing sugar or arranging orange slices on top, if you like.

White chocolate-raspberry cheesecake

Serves 10

Ingredients

175g digestive biscuits
125g unsalted butter
200g white chocolate chips
200g cream cheese
100g caster sugar
4 eggs, plus 2 egg yolks
50g plain flour
½ vanilla pod, seeds scraped out
275g raspberries, plus more to serve
10g mint leaves, to serve

Method

Line the base and sides of a 25cm springform tart tin with baking parchment. Put the digestives in a food processor or blender and blitz to crumbs, or seal them into a sturdy freezer bag and bash with a rolling pin for a little stress relief and the same result. Melt the butter in a saucepan and mix with the crumbs. Press them into the prepared tin to form a dense layer. Chill.

Preheat the oven to 180°C/fan 160°C/350°F/gas 4. Put the chocolate in a heatproof bowl over simmering water. Make sure the bowl does not touch the water. Beat the cream cheese and sugar, then beat in the eggs and extra egg yolks gradually. Mix in the flour and vanilla seeds, then add the melted chocolate slowly, stirring, until well mixed.

Place a layer of raspberries on the base and pour on the chocolate mixture. Bake until it sets 7.5cm from the edge but the centre is wobbly (45–55 minutes). Run a knife around the rim, cool, then chill. When ready to serve, remove carefully from the tin. Serve with more raspberries and the mint leaves.

Saffron and cardamom crème brûlée

Cyrus Todiwala, OBE, DL, Clink Chef Ambassador

Here we have an internationally popular dessert, the addition of saffron and cardamom giving it my own particular stamp. For an even more sophisticated version, soak the sugar in neutral alcohol, such as vodka, before flaming it.

Serves 4

Ingredients

250ml creamy whole milk, preferably non-homogenised

40g fresh root ginger, unpeeled and roughly chopped

4–5 cardamom pods, lightly crushed

450ml double cream

a few drops of vanilla extract

6 egg yolks

about 150g caster sugar

good pinch of powdered saffron, or to taste

Method

Preheat the oven to 150°C/fan 130°C/300°F/gas 2 and find 4 x 150ml ramekins. Put the milk, ginger and cardamom into a heavy-based saucepan and bring gently to the boil. Reduce the heat and simmer until the milk has reduced by about three-quarters to 100ml. Keep scraping the sides of the pan during this reduction to prevent wastage and burning. Allow to cool slightly, then transfer to a blender and whizz to a purée. Pass through a sieve, using the back of a spoon to press all the milk into a bowl. (Discard the solids, or use them to make tea.)

Return the milk to the pan, add the cream and bring to a simmer. Stir in the vanilla and slowly return to a simmer. Meanwhile, put the egg yolks and 115g of the caster sugar into a bowl and whisk until frothy. Beat in the cream mixture. Return it to the pan and stir over a gentle heat for 1–2 minutes, until the sugar dissolves. Add the saffron, a bit at a time, until quite deep yellow. Pour into the ramekins. Place in a baking tray and pour in hot water to come halfway up the sides. Bake for 30–35 minutes, until firm but with a slight wobble in the centre. Cool, then chill.

When ready to serve, preheat the grill on its highest setting, or get out a kitchen blowtorch. Sprinkle half the remaining sugar over the ramekins. Heat under the grill or with the blowtorch until a layer of caramel forms. Sprinkle the rest of the sugar over and grill or blowtorch again to form a thick, crunchy layer. Serve immediately, so that the brûlée topping is still crisp.

Chocolate mousse with marshmallow ice

Kerry Rickett, Clink Head Chef Trainer, HMP Styal

Serves 6

Ingredients

For the mousse

40g unsalted butter
250g good-quality milk
  chocolate, broken up
6 eggs, plus 2 egg whites
pinch of salt

For the walnut praline

100g caster sugar
50g walnuts, finely chopped

**For the marshmallow
  ice cream**

1 litre double cream
200g can of sweetened
  condensed milk
100g (½ jar) of
  marshmallow fluff

Method

First, make the chocolate mousse. Melt the butter and chocolate over a low heat, stirring constantly. Once smooth, remove from the heat, pour into a large bowl and leave to cool slightly. Separate the eggs and add each egg yolk to the chocolate mixture individually, stirring vigorously after each is added, so the yolks don't get hot.

Place all 8 egg whites into a separate bowl, add a pinch of salt and whisk until really stiff. Add a spoonful of egg white to the chocolate mixture and stir so that the chocolate becomes slightly more runny. Add the remaining egg whites in 3 parts, gently folding them in with a wooden spoon or silicone spatula. You want it to remain nicely fluffy, so don't beat it.

Once all the egg whites are incorporated, pour the mousse into 6 small bowls or glasses, cover with cling film and place in the fridge for 3 hours or overnight.

For the praline, line a baking tray with baking parchment. Put the sugar in a saucepan with 2 tbsp water, place over a low heat and stir for about 5 minutes until the sugar has dissolved. Increase the heat to high and bring to the boil without stirring, until the mixture turns golden. Remove from the heat and set aside for 3 minutes to allow the bubbles to subside. Add the walnuts and pour the caramel out on to the prepared tray. Allow to cool and set, then break up or chop into small pieces.

For the ice cream, in a mixing bowl, whip the cream until stiff peaks form. Blend in the condensed milk and fluff. Pour into a loaf tin lined with cling film and freeze until solid.

Serve the mousse with the ice cream and walnut praline shards, sprinkling with praline rubble.

Al's nougat semifreddo

Serves 8

Ingredients

3 eggs, separated
2 tbsp caster sugar
250g mascarpone cheese
100g crunchy nougat,
   chopped by hand
chopped candied fruits and
   crushed hazelnuts, to serve

Method

Whisk the egg whites in a bowl until stiff. Put the yolks and sugar in another bowl and beat until fluffy. Add the mascarpone and keep beating. Add the chopped nougat and fold in the beaten egg whites.

Line a rectangular mould or loaf tin, about 20 x 10cm, with baking parchment or cling film. Pour the mixture into the mould. Freeze for 2–3 hours.

Unmould the semifreddo on a serving dish and decorate with candied fruits and hazelnuts. Serve immediately.

Lemon cream flan
Alison Hulm, Clink Administration Manager

Serves 6

Ingredients

85g unsalted butter,
   or margarine
175g digestive biscuits
150ml double cream
175g condensed milk
juice of 2 lemons

Method

Melt the butter or margarine in a saucepan. Meanwhile, put the biscuits in a freezer bag, seal, then bash with a rolling pin until you have crumbs. Mix well into the melted butter. Press into a 20cm flan dish, making a compact layer on the base and going a little way up the sides.

Whip the cream until billowing but not at all stiff. Add the condensed milk and whip again, this time until the mixture is stiff. Gradually add the lemon juice. Spoon on to the base and smooth the top. Serve chilled.

Pineapple mousse with Merlyn jelly
John Retallick, Clink Chef Ambassador

Serves 10

Ingredients

For the mousse

1 large or 2 small pineapples, finely sliced into rings

8 eggs, separated

200g caster sugar

finely grated zest and juice of 2 unwaxed lemons

pineapple extract (optional)

350ml double cream

500g finely chopped pineapple

For the jelly

200g caster sugar

100ml Merlyn liqueur

3 leaves of gelatine

Method

Preheat the oven to 150°C/fan 130°C/300°F/gas 2. Place the finely sliced pineapple on baking parchment on a wire rack, place in the oven and leave to dry slowly.

Place the egg yolks, sugar and lemon zest and juice in a heatproof bowl over a saucepan of simmering water (don't let the bowl touch the water). Whisk over the heat until it thickens. Remove from the heat and add pineapple extract to taste (if using). Separately whip the cream to soft peaks, then carefully mix it into the mousse. Whisk the egg whites until stiff and fold them in, too. Place the finely chopped pineapple into a large mousse mould, or 10 glasses, then add the mousse and chill to set.

Meanwhile, make the jelly. Bring 200ml water to the boil with the sugar, stirring until the sugar dissolves. Stir in the liqueur and remove from the heat. Soak the gelatine leaves in cold water to just-cover for 5 minutes. Squeeze out the excess water and stir into the warm liqueur mixture until it dissolves. Cover the mousse with the Merlyn jelly and chill once more, to set.

Decorate with the dried pineapple slices to serve.

Puddings and Cakes

Chocolate and cherry tart

This also works well with peeled, sliced pears instead of cherries.

Serves 10

Ingredients

For the pastry

200g plain flour, plus more to dust

25g semolina

1 tbsp caster sugar

100g unsalted butter, chopped

1 egg, lightly beaten

For the filling

100g caster sugar

140g ground almonds

140g unsalted butter, melted

1 egg, plus 1 egg yolk

40g dark chocolate chips

500g fresh cherries, pitted,
    or canned cherries

Method

Mix the plain flour, semolina and sugar in a large bowl, or a food processor. If making by hand, add the butter and rub the mixture together with your fingertips until it resembles breadcrumbs. If using a food processor, blitz, using the pulse button. Mix in the egg until the pastry comes together in a ball. Knead lightly into a disc, wrap in cling film and refrigerate for 30 minutes.

When ready to bake, lightly dust a work surface with flour and preheat the oven to 180°C/fan 160°C/350°F/gas 4. Roll out the pastry to 5mm thick. Use it to line a 25cm diameter tart tin. Line the pastry case with baking parchment and fill with baking beans, or raw rice (see page 83). Blind-bake for 15–20 minutes, or until the pastry looks dry on top. Leave to cool.

Preheat the oven again, this time to 190°C/fan 170°C/375°F/gas 5. Mix the first 4 filling ingredients, fold in the chocolate chips, spread over the pastry and top with the cherries.

Bake for 25 minutes, then leave to cool before serving.

Panettone pudding

Serves 8

Ingredients

50g unsalted butter
½ panettone or pandoro, as you prefer, cut into 2cm slices
3 egg yolks
500ml single cream
Demerara sugar, to sprinkle on top

Method

Preheat the oven to 160°C/fan 140°C/325°F/gas 3. Spread the butter evenly over an ovenproof pie dish that is big enough to fit all the panettone or pandoro into, making sure you push the butter right into the corners. Or use individual dishes, if you prefer. Line with slices of panettone.

Whisk the egg yolks and add the cream, mixing well. Pour the egg mixture into the dish or dishes, covering the panettone or pandoro evenly. Sprinkle the sugar on top.

Bake for 40 minutes for a large pudding, or 20–25 minutes for smaller puddings. Serve hot or cold, with cream.

Finlay's chocolate, prune and cognac cake
Finlay Scott, Clink Chairman and Founder Trustee

Serves 8

Ingredients

400g pitted prunes
120ml cognac
6 large eggs, separated
150g golden caster sugar
50g cocoa powder
unsalted butter, for the tin
2 tbsp crème fraîche
150g 70% cocoa solids dark chocolate, broken up

Method

The night before, soak the prunes in the cognac in a small bowl.

Next day, preheat the oven to 180°C/fan 160°C/350°F/gas 4. Put the egg whites and yolks into separate clean bowls. Add the sugar to the yolks and whisk until light and fluffy; do not over-whisk, 2–3 minutes and no more. Fold in the cocoa. Whisk the egg whites until stiff. Using a large spoon, slowly, and taking care not to beat the air out, fold the egg whites into the chocolate mixture a bit at a time (3 times should suffice).

Butter 2 x 20cm sandwich tins and line with silicone paper. Divide the batter between them. Bake for 15 minutes, leave to cool, then carefully remove from the tins and peel off the papers.

Choose 8 of the biggest prunes, then put the rest, with the cognac, in a food processor with half the crème fraîche. Blend to a purée. Use the purée to cover one of the sponges, then place the other sponge on top to form a sandwich.

For the topping, place the chocolate in a heatproof bowl over a saucepan of simmering water. Make sure the bowl is not touching the water. Once the chocolate is smooth and shiny, allow to cool slightly, then mix in the remaining crème fraîche. Using a palette knife, spread the chocolate over the cake and finish with the reserved prunes.

Bolo rei – 'King's cake'
Cyrus Todiwala, OBE, DL, Clink Chef Ambassador

This is fit for a king, and dates from a time when pistachios were rare and expensive, so enjoyed only by the elite. The cake mixture can also be used to make biscuits.

Makes 20 bite-sized pieces

Ingredients

375g unsalted butter, softened
375g caster sugar
5 eggs, plus 4 egg yolks
250g plain flour
1 tsp baking powder
½ tsp salt
125g fine semolina
300g ground almonds
300g ground pistachios
finely ground seeds from 10–12 cardamom pods
1 tsp vanilla extract

For the topping

250g white chocolate, broken up
50g ground pistachios

Method

Preheat the oven to 160°C/fan 140°C/325°F/gas 3. Line a 30cm square cake tin with greaseproof paper.

Beat the butter and sugar until smooth and creamy. Mix in the eggs and yolks, but don't beat them in. Sift in the flour, baking powder and salt and stir well. Mix in the semolina, ground nuts and cardamom, then add the vanilla.

Pour into the prepared tin and bake for 10 minutes. Reduce the oven temperature to 140°C/fan 120°C/275°F/gas 1 and bake for a further 40–50 minutes, until a skewer comes out clean. Leave to cool. The cake is crumbly and delicate, so carefully turn it out, peel off the paper and place on a rack.

To make the topping, melt the chocolate in a heatproof bowl over simmering water (make sure the bowl does not touch the water). Take off the heat and mix in the ground pistachios, then pour over the cake. Leave to set, then cut into small squares and present in mini paper cases.

Waldorf pudding
Daniel Ayton, Clink Chef Ambassador

Ingredients

2 large tart apples, peeled
and cored
5 tbsp sultanas
2 tbsp lemon juice
1 tbsp crystallised ginger,
finely chopped
1 tbsp unsalted butter
4 tbsp granulated sugar
480ml double cream
1 tsp vanilla extract
5 egg yolks, lightly beaten
pinch of ground nutmeg
2 tbsp halved walnuts

Method

Preheat the oven to 160°C/fan 140°C/325°F/gas 3. Thinly slice the apples, add the sultanas, lemon and ginger. Melt the butter over a high heat, add the apples and cook for 1 minute. Stir in half the sugar. Stir for 3–4 minutes, or until lightly caramelised. Scrape into 8 ramekins or 6 teacups.

Meanwhile, over a medium heat, bring the cream and vanilla to a simmer, stirring, until bubbles form round the edge. Whisk the remaining sugar with the egg yolks, beat in some of the cream, then stir in the remaining cream. Pour over the apples and sprinkle with nutmeg. Set the dishes in a roasting tin, then pour boiling water into the tin to come halfway up the sides of the dishes. Bake for 20–25 minutes, or until the custard has set. Sprinkle with walnuts and serve at room temperature.

Bread pudding

Serves 5

Ingredients

225g stale bread
½ tsp mixed spice
100g brown sugar
110g sultanas
1 egg, lightly beaten
100ml whole milk
unsalted butter, for the dish

Method

Preheat the oven to 170°C/fan 150°C/340°F/gas 3½. Tear the bread into small pieces, place in a bowl and cover with cold water. Leave to soak for 1 hour. Squeeze out as much water as possible, then put into a large bowl and mash well. Mix in the mixed spice, 75g of the sugar and the sultanas, then the egg, gradually adding milk to make it sticky but not wet.

Pour into a well-buttered baking dish and sprinkle with the remaining sugar. Bake for 1 hour, or until a knife comes out clean. Cover with baking parchment to stop it burning, if needed. Serve hot or cold, with custard (see page 59).

Raspberry Bakewell tart

Serves 10

Ingredients

For the pastry

200g plain flour, plus more
to dust
25g semolina
1 tbsp caster sugar
100g unsalted butter, chopped
1 egg, lightly beaten

For the filling

140g caster sugar
140g ground almonds
140g unsalted butter, melted
1 egg, plus 1 egg yolk
2 punnets of raspberries
180g clotted cream

Method

Make the pastry as on page 73. Knead lightly into a disc, wrap in cling film and refrigerate for 30 minutes.

When ready to bake, lightly dust a work surface with flour and preheat the oven to 180°C/fan 160°C/350°F/gas 4. Roll out the pastry to 5mm thick. Use it to line a 25cm diameter tart tin. Line with baking parchment and fill with baking beans, or raw rice. Blind bake for 15–20 minutes (see opposite), or until it looks dry on top. Leave to cool.

Preheat the oven again to 190°C/fan 170°C/375°F/gas 5.

Mix together the caster sugar, ground almonds, butter, egg and egg yolk. Place most of the raspberries in a layer over the pastry and spread the almond mixture on top.

Bake for 25–35 minutes. Leave until just at room temperature, then serve with more raspberries, and the clotted cream.

Step-by-step
Blind baking pastry

STEP ONE
This ensures a crisp pastry base. Make the pastry as directed, then roll it over a rolling pin and unroll it over a tart tin. Press it into the corners, but leave the edges untrimmed, in case of shrinkage. Prick the base with a fork.

STEP TWO
Make a large circle of baking parchment, then fold it into a triangle and cut into it at 1cm intervals. Unfold it and use to line the pastry; the cuts will allow it to fit perfectly.

STEP THREE
Fill the baking-parchment lined pastry with porcelain baking beans, or dried beans, or raw rice. These will act as weights and prevent the pastry from rising.

STEP FOUR
Bake for the time instructed by the recipe. The pastry will cook beneath the baking parchment; you should see that it appears sandy and looks dry when it is ready. Remove the baking beans and parchment and proceed as directed by the recipe.

Malva pudding with orange caramel sauce
Daniel Ayton, Clink Chef Ambassador

Makes 6

Ingredients

For the sauce

250ml double cream
100g unsalted butter
125g Demerara sugar
25ml orange juice,
   sherry, whisky or brandy

For the pudding

2 eggs
250g caster sugar
15g apricot jam
1 tsp white wine vinegar
30g unsalted butter
125ml whole milk
315g plain flour
1 tsp bicarbonate of soda
salt

Method

For the sauce, boil all the ingredients together, then cool.

Preheat the oven to 180°C/fan 160°C/350°F/gas 4.

Beat the eggs and sugar with the jam until fluffy. Meanwhile, melt the vinegar with the butter and milk, then cool slightly. Sift the dry ingredients together.

Fold the dry ingredients and the butter mixture alternately into the egg mixture. Pour into 6 individual pudding basins, place them in a roasting tin for stability, then bake for 10–15 minutes.

When the puddings come out of the oven, leave them to rest for 5 minutes, then prick all over with a skewer and spoon a little sauce over each to soak in.

To serve, turn out of the dishes, pour over the remaining sauce and serve with crème fraîche, to cut through the sweetness.

Spotted dick

Serves 5

Ingredients

300g plain flour
2 tsp baking powder
150g shredded vegetable suet
75g caster sugar
125g currants
finely grated zest of
    1 unwaxed lemon
200ml whole milk
10g unsalted butter

Method

Put the flour, baking powder, suet, sugar, currants and lemon zest in a bowl and mix. Stir in the milk to make a soft dough.

Butter 5 individual pudding basins, then divide the mixture between them. It should fill each two-thirds of the way. Cover with small rounds of baking parchment, pleated in the centre, and tie it to the basins with string.

Bring a large steamer to the boil. Steam the puddings for 1 hour. Remove the papers and turn the puddings on to plates. Serve with custard, sit back and wait for the plaudits!

Caribbean molasses cake
Sir William Atkinson, Clink Trustee

Serves 8

Ingredients

75g unsalted butter or margarine,
  plus more for the tin
50g brown sugar
120ml molasses
100g raisins or sultanas
220g plain flour
¼ tsp ground ginger
1 tsp salt
¼ tbsp bicarbonate of soda
1 tbsp baking powder
¼ tsp ground cinnamon
1 egg, lightly beaten

Method

Preheat the oven to 180°C/fan 160°C/350°F/gas 4. Lightly butter a 20cm round, deep cake tin.

Place 120ml water in a small saucepan, bring to the boil, then remove from the heat. Add the butter or margarine and stir to melt, then add the sugar and molasses, mixing well, then stir in the raisins or sultanas. Set aside.

Sift the flour, ginger, salt, bicarbonate of soda, baking powder and cinnamon together in a large bowl. Add the egg and the liquid in the saucepan and mix to a thin batter.

Transfer to the prepared tin and bake for 30–40 minutes. Cool on a wire rack.

Gluten-free chocolate cake
Debbie Whitworth, Clink Finance Director

Serves 8

Ingredients

170g unsalted butter,
plus more for the tin
225g dark chocolate
broken up
170g light brown sugar
6 eggs, separated
½ tsp vanilla extract
2 tbsp rice flour
2 tbsp potato flour

Method

Preheat the oven to 180°C/fan 160°C/350°F/gas 4. Butter a 23cm round cake tin, or loaf tin, and line with baking parchment.

Melt the chocolate, butter and sugar in a large heatproof bowl over simmering water (make sure the bowl does not touch the water). Allow to cool a little. Mix in the yolks one at a time, but don't beat. Add the vanilla and sift in both flours. Whisk the egg whites until stiff. Gently fold into the batter, being careful not to knock out the air. It doesn't have to be perfectly mixed; the odd bit of egg white won't matter as much as over-mixing.

Pour into the tin and bake for 30 minutes. Check after about 25 minutes. This is a rich, damp, brownie-like cake, so you want quite a few gungy bits on the testing knife.

Gluten-free lemon and chocolate chip cake
Debbie Whitworth, Clink Finance Director

Serves 8

Ingredients

For the cake

100g unsalted butter,
   melted, plus more for the tin
200g caster sugar
125g cream cheese
3 eggs
100g ground almonds
finely grated zest of
   3 unwaxed lemons,
   plus 1 tbsp lemon juice
½ tsp vanilla extract
125g dark chocolate chips
110g rice flour
40g potato flour
½ tsp xanthan gum
2 tsp baking powder

For the icing

finely grated zest of
   1 unwaxed lemon,
   plus 3 tbsp lemon juice
150g icing sugar
apricot jam, to glaze

Method

Preheat the oven to 180°C/fan 160°C/350°F/gas 4. Butter a 17cm-long loaf tin and line the base with baking parchment. Mix together the butter and caster sugar, then beat in the cream cheese until smooth. Beat in the eggs one at a time.

Beat in the almonds, lemon zest and vanilla. Stir in the chocolate chips and lemon juice. Sift in the flours, xanthan gum and baking powder and gently fold in. Pour into the prepared tin and bake for 60–70 minutes. There should be a few crumbs sticking to the knife when you test it, so it remains moist. Don't turn off the oven.

Turn out the cake on to a wire rack and place a large plate underneath it. Leave to cool for 10 minutes. Gently heat the lemon zest, juice and icing sugar in a small pan. Warm the jam and spread a thin layer over the cake. Leave for 5 minutes to set a bit, then spoon the lemon glaze over.

Place on a baking tray and put it in the oven. Turn off the oven and leave the cake in there for about 4 minutes; this should make the glaze translucent.

Butterscotch pudding with whisky sauce
Matt Tebbutt, Clink Chef Ambassador

I've used walnuts and prunes in this one. If that is not your thing, just leave them out. The whisky sauce, however, is essential to the decadence of the dish. Serve with lots of thick double cream.

Serves 8

Ingredients

For the pudding

50g unsalted butter, softened, plus more for the tin

60g light brown sugar

1 vanilla pod, split and seeds scraped out

2 tsp baking powder

225g self-raising flour

pinch of bicarbonate of soda

2 eggs

300ml whole milk, warmed

50g walnuts, chopped, plus more to serve (optional)

50g prunes, pitted and chopped

For the sauce

85g unsalted butter

85g muscovado sugar

200ml double cream

whisky, to taste

Method

Preheat the oven to 180°C/fan 160°C/350°F/gas 4. Butter a 20cm square baking tin.

Beat the butter, sugar and vanilla seeds in a bowl. In another bowl, mix the baking powder with the flour and bicarbonate of soda. Lightly beat the eggs in a third bowl. Slowly and alternately add small amounts of flour and egg to the butter mixture. Do not over-beat as this will toughen the gluten and produce a dense pudding. Add the milk to form a sloppy batter, then stir in the nuts and prunes. Pour into the prepared tin and bake for 30–40 minutes, or until firm.

To make the sauce, boil the butter and sugar together for 5 minutes. Pour in the cream, return to the boil, then add a capful of whisky or 2 to taste.

Cut a wedge of the pudding and coat liberally with the sauce, sprinkling with more walnuts, if you like.

Chocolates, Sweets and Biscuits

Hazelnut biscotti

Ingredients

250g plain flour, plus more
   to dust
½ tsp baking powder
250g caster sugar
3 eggs, lightly beaten
200g chopped hazelnuts

Method

Preheat the oven to 170°C/fan 150°C/340°F/gas 3½. Line a large baking tray with baking parchment.

Mix the flour, baking powder and sugar in a bowl and add the eggs gradually, then mix in the nuts. On a floured surface, knead the mixture and divide into 2. Roll each into a 25cm log, place on the lined baking tray and bake for 25 minutes.

Remove from the oven, leave to cool slightly, then cut each log into 1½–2cm-thick slices. Lay the slices on the baking tray.

Return the tray to the oven and bake for another 5–7 minutes, turn over and continue to bake for another 5–7 minutes until golden brown. Remove from the oven and cool on a wire rack.

Ginger biscuits

Makes 25

Ingredients

110g unsalted butter,
   plus more for the tray
110g caster sugar
110g golden syrup
225g self-raising flour,
   plus more to dust
2 tsp ground ginger

Method

Preheat the oven to 180°C/fan 160°C/350°F/gas 4. Lightly butter a baking tray.

Melt the butter, caster sugar and golden syrup in a pan over a gentle heat. When melted, remove from the heat and cool slightly. Add the flour and ginger.

When cool enough to handle, with floured hands, roll the dough into golf ball-sized balls. Place these on the prepared baking tray with enough room between each to allow them to spread during cooking. Mark the top of each ball with a fork.

Bake for 10–12 minutes, or until golden brown.

Remove from the oven, leave to cool slightly, then transfer to a wire rack with a palette knife. Leave until cold.

Chilli chocolate rum truffles

Makes 50

Ingredients

450g good-quality dark
  chocolate, broken up
50g unsalted butter
2 tbsp rum
pinch of chilli powder
2 tsp single cream

For coating and decorating

300g good-quality dark
  chocolate
150g white chocolate
pinch of chilli flakes

Method

Put the chocolate and butter in a large heatproof bowl and place over a saucepan of simmering water until all the chocolate has melted. (Be sure the bowl does not touch the water.) Add the rum, chilli and cream. Mix well, pour into a container and leave to cool completely.

Roll into balls, place on a tray and chill in the fridge until set.

Now melt the dark chocolate to coat the truffles, in the same way as before. Spear each truffle with a narrow skewer and dip into the dark chocolate, then place on a tray lined with baking parchment. Once cooled, melt the white chocolate as before, then drizzle it over the truffles with a fork to decorate. Scatter cautiously with chilli flakes. Leave to set, then serve.

Membrillo

Makes 6 x 300g jars, or a 1.8kg slab

Ingredients

1.8kg quince, chopped, core
and all
800g–1kg granulated sugar,
plus more to coat
juice of 1 lemon, or to taste

Method

Put the quince in a saucepan with 2 litres water. Bring to the boil over a high heat, then reduce to a simmer, cover and simmer for 45 minutes. Mash the quince and water. Pour into a jelly bag or piece of muslin inside a bowl. Tie up with string and hang over the bowl overnight. Don't be tempted to squeeze it, or it will become cloudy.

Measure the liquid. For every 250ml, add 200g sugar. Place in a large pan over a low heat, stirring until it boils. Boil for 25 minutes, adding the lemon juice to sharpen the mixture in the final stages. Put 1 tsp on a chilled saucer. If, when you push it, it wrinkles, setting point has been reached. Pour into a dish, to lie 2cm thick. Cool, then chill overnight. Cut into cubes and roll in sugar to serve as a sweetmeat.

Salted butter caramels

You will need a sugar thermometer.

Makes 22

Ingredients
250ml whipping cream
75g unsalted butter, cut into 4
1 tsp sea salt flakes,
   plus more to serve
300g granulated sugar
50g golden syrup

Method
Line a 20cm square baking tin with baking parchment. In a small saucepan, bring the cream, butter and salt to a simmer. Once the butter has melted and the cream starts to bubble, remove from the heat. In a second saucepan over a medium heat, bring the sugar, golden syrup and 60ml water to the boil, stirring to dissolve the sugar. Continue cooking, carefully swirling the pan, until the mixture is a uniform medium caramel colour. Gently pour in the hot cream mixture. The mixture will bubble up, so keep stirring to stop it boiling over. Cook, stirring often, until it reaches 116°C (241°F), or forms a slightly firm ball when a teaspoon of it is dropped into ice-cold water.

Pour into the prepared tin and cool for 2–3 hours at room temperature. Scatter with sea salt flakes and cut into squares to serve, in bonbon wrappers or petits fours cases, if you like.

Quick macaroons

Makes 20

Ingredients
5 large egg whites
350g caster sugar
160g ground almonds
a little flavourless oil

Method
Preheat the oven to 160°C/fan 140°C/325°F/gas 3.

Whisk the egg whites to stiff peaks. Gradually add the sugar, still beating, then carefully fold in the almonds with a spoon. Put the mixture into a piping bag. Lightly oil a baking tray or sheet. Pipe 4cm rounds of the mixture on to the oiled tray.

Bake for 10 minutes, then leave to cool on a wire rack.

Chocolate chip cookies

Makes 30

Ingredients

250g unsalted butter, softened
250g light brown sugar
125g caster sugar
2 eggs
½ tsp vanilla extract
500g self-raising flour
375g chocolate chips

Method

Cream the butter and both sugars together until light and fluffy. Add the eggs gradually, beating until fully incorporated, then add the vanilla. Tip in the flour and mix well, then add the chocolate chips gradually until evenly distributed.

Divide into 4 and roll each into a 3cm-thick sausage. Wrap in cling film and leave in the fridge for 2 hours (or you can also freeze the dough at this point, if it's more convenient).

Preheat the oven to 160°C/fan 140°C/325°F/gas 3. Remove the cling film from the cookie dough and cut it into 5mm-thick rounds. Place each on a lined baking tray, making sure there is plenty of room between them as they will spread.

Bake for 12 minutes, then try to leave to cool on a wire rack before eating!

Pistachio tuiles

Kerry Rickett, Clink Head Chef Trainer, HMP Styal

Makes about 20

Ingredients

30g pistachios
20g ground almonds
2 egg whites
75g caster sugar
10g plain flour

Method

Preheat the oven to 150°C/fan 130°C/300°F/gas 2.

Grind the pistachios in a food processor until they have a similar consistency to the ground almonds. Place in a bowl with all the other ingredients and mix thoroughly.

Lay a non-stick silicone mat on a baking sheet and pour the mixture on it, spreading it as thinly as you can; it should be about 2mm thick. Bake for 10–15 minutes until golden (you want to keep the pale-green pistachio colour).

Leave to set, then break into shards to serve.

Churros and chocolate sauce

Makes 20

Ingredients

For the churros

50g salted butter, melted, plus 1 tsp

½ tsp vanilla extract

1 tsp baking powder

300g plain flour, plus more if needed

pinch of salt

sunflower oil, or other flavourless vegetable oil, to deep-fry

75g caster sugar

1 tsp ground cinnamon

For the sauce

200g good-quality dark chocolate, broken up or chopped

100ml double cream

100ml whole milk

2 tbsp golden syrup

Method

For the churros, pour 350ml water into a saucepan and bring it to the boil. Add the butter and vanilla. Put the baking powder, flour and salt into a large bowl.

Make a well in the centre of the flour mixture and pour in the water mixture all at once, beating vigorously with a wooden spoon until smooth and fairly firm. It needs to be pipe-able without streaming out of the piping nozzle, so add a little more flour to the mix if necessary. Set aside for 10 minutes.

To make the sauce, put the chocolate, cream, milk and syrup into a heavy-based saucepan and place over a medium-low heat to melt slowly. Once you have a smooth chocolate sauce, keep it warm.

Heat about 10cm oil in a large saucepan or deep-fat fryer to 160°C (320°C). If you don't have a thermometer, a piece of the churros dough carefully dropped in should turn golden in 25–30 seconds. Place the dough in a piping bag fitted with a 2cm star-shaped nozzle.

Pipe 3–4 strips straight into the oil, using a pair of kitchen scissors to cut each to about 10cm long. Fry until golden brown. Scoop out with a slotted spoon and drain on kitchen paper. Keep warm while you fry the rest in the same way.

Mix the caster sugar and cinnamon together and use it to dust the warm churros. Serve with the warm chocolate sauce, dipping the churros into the sauce as you eat.

Tangy lemon marshmallows

Makes 20 large marshmallows

Ingredients

100ml lemon juice
2 x 12g sachets of powdered gelatine
450g caster sugar
150ml golden syrup
a little flavourless vegetable oil
50g icing sugar
2 tbsp cornflour
finely grated zest of 1 unwaxed lemon

Method

Line a 20cm square tin with cling film, leaving an overhang.

Pour the lemon juice into the bowl of a food mixer and sprinkle in the gelatine. Leave the gelatine to soften and absorb the liquid.

Meanwhile, put the caster sugar, golden syrup and 150ml water in a saucepan. Cook over a low heat, stirring all the time, until the sugar has dissolved, then quickly bring to the boil. Using a sugar thermometer, boil until the syrup reaches 130°C (266°F), then remove from the heat. Leave to cool until it stops bubbling.

Whisk the gelatine mixture in the food mixer on a medium speed. Add the sugar syrup, slowly pouring it down the side of the mixer bowl. (Try not to pour it directly on to the whisk to avoid getting lumps of sugar in the marshmallow.) The marshmallow mixture should become pale and grow in volume like a stiff meringue. Once all the syrup has been added, continue to whisk for 5–10 minutes, or until the marshmallow is really thick and cools a bit more. It is ready when the outside of the bowl is only slightly warm and the marshmallow starts to get really sticky.

Using an oiled spatula, scrape it into the prepared tin, keeping the spatula clean. Leave to set at room temperature for 1–2 hours, or until firm.

Sift the icing sugar and cornflour together into a small bowl and stir in the lemon zest. Use some of this mixture to coat the top of the marshmallow. Using the cling film overhang to lift the marshmallow up, then remove it from the tin. Cut it into 4cm cubes, then dust each cube in the remaining icing sugar and zest mixture. Serve.

Chocolate-coated peppermint creams

Makes about 30

Ingredients

1 egg white
juice of ½ lemon
1 tsp peppermint extract
425g icing sugar, plus more to dust
175g dark chocolate, broken up

Method

Whisk the egg white in a bowl until it forms stiff peaks. Slowly whisk in the lemon juice, peppermint and icing sugar to a stiff paste. Put the peppermint mixture on to a work surface dusted with icing sugar and roll it out to about 5mm thick.

Use a 5cm cutter — any shape you have — to cut out the sweets and put them on a tray or plate. Put in the fridge for 2 hours, or until they have set.

While the sweets are setting, melt the chocolate in a heatproof bowl over a pan of simmering water, taking care that the bowl doesn't touch the water, or temper the chocolate for a shiny finish (see right).

Dip each peppermint into the chocolate and put on a plate or tray. Return to the fridge until the chocolate has set.

Step-by-step
Tempering chocolate

STEP ONE
Chop three-quarters of the chocolate and melt in a heatproof bowl over a saucepan of simmering water. Finely chop the remaining one-quarter.

STEP TWO
Check the temperature with a thermometer. When it reaches 55–58°C for dark chocolate, or 45–50°C for milk or white chocolate, remove the bowl from the saucepan. Set aside one-third in a warm place.

STEP THREE
Add the finely chopped chocolate to the remaining melted chocolate, stirring constantly, until the temperature is 28–29°C for dark chocolate; 27–28°C for milk chocolate, or 26–27°C for white chocolate.

STEP FOUR
Return the melted chocolate that you set aside at the end of step two. The temperature should climb to 31–32°C for dark chocolate, 29–30°C for milk chocolate, or 28–29°C for white chocolate. Stir constantly untill the temperature is reached. If it reaches the right temperature at any point and there are still pieces of unmelted chocolate, remove them. The tempered chocolate, once set, will be shiny and have a crisp 'snap' when broken or bitten into.

Ann Elliott's flapjack
Liz Elliott, Clink Support Worker, HMP High Down

A crazily easy flapjack recipe my mum used to make us. So simple!

Makes 16

Ingredients

150g margarine or unsalted
   butter, plus more for the tin
1–2 tbsp golden syrup
100g Demerara sugar
200g porridge oats
1 tsp almond or vanilla extract

Method

Preheat the oven to 180°C/fan 160°C/350°F/gas 4. Butter a 30 x 20cm ovenproof dish and line it with baking parchment.

Melt the margarine or butter, syrup and sugar in a saucepan. Stir in the oats and almond or vanilla extract and spread the mixture evenly into the prepared tin.

Bake for 20 minutes, or until golden brown. Leave to cool in the tin, then cut into squares to serve.

Al's chocolate chip amaretti

Great with *un bel espresso*. This recipe can be made without the chocolate chips for a more authentic (but less indulgent) amaretti biscuit.

Makes 20

Ingredients

unsalted butter,
    for the baking sheet
4 egg whites
340g caster sugar
340g ground almonds
30ml amaretto liqueur
30g dark chocolate chips

Method

Preheat the oven to 170°C/fan 150°C/340°F/gas 3½. Butter a baking sheet and line it with baking parchment.

In a bowl, whisk the egg whites until firm. Fold in the sugar and almonds gently, taking care not to beat the air out. Fold in the amaretto gently until you have a smooth paste.

Using a teaspoon, place small heaps of the mixture about 3cm apart on the prepared baking sheet. They will expand while cooking. Place 3 small chocolate chips on top of each.

Bake for 15 minutes, or until golden brown. Leave to cool.

Espresso and walnut brownies
Matt Tebbutt, Clink Chef Ambassador

Serves 6

Ingredients

150g unsalted butter, softened, plus more, melted, for the tin

200g toasted and chopped walnuts, plus ground walnuts for the tin

300g good-quality dark chocolate, broken up

150g soft brown sugar

4 eggs

100g raisins, softened in 30ml hot espresso for 30 minutes

150g mascarpone cheese

1 espresso cup of espresso grind (fine) coffee powder

30ml shot of espresso coffee

Method

Brush a cake tin or suitable dish first with melted butter and then dust with ground walnuts, to prevent the brownie from sticking. Preheat the oven to 150°C/fan 130°C/300°F/gas 2.

Melt the chocolate in a heatproof bowl over a saucepan of simmering water (make sure the bowl does not touch the water). Leave to cool slightly. Meanwhile, in a food mixer, beat the butter and sugar until pale. Slowly add each egg, alternating with the raisins and their remaining liquid, and the walnuts.

At this point the mix will look horribly split, but don't panic, because it will all come together when the chocolate is added. Beat in the mascarpone, espresso grind and coffee shot.

Finally add the cooled chocolate. Pour into the prepared tin and bake for 25–30 minutes or until a crack appears round the inside surface. Allow to cool. Serve at room temperature with scoops of good-quality ice cream.

First published in Great Britain in 2017 by The Clink Trading

A CIP catalogue record for this title is available from the British Library
ISBN 978-0-9933569-2-6

Publisher: Alison Cathie
Editor: Lucy Bannell
Photography and design: Ros Holder
Foreword (pages 4–5) and jacket flap portrait photography:
David Cummings
Home Economist: Nicola Roberts
Proofreader: Joanne Murray
Indexer: Vicki Robinson
PR and marketing: Custard Communications
Project manager: Christopher Moore

Printed and bound in China by 1010 Printing International Limited

The Clink Trading
HMP High Down
High Down Lane
Sutton
Surrey
SM2 5PJ

www.theclinkcharity.org

Tiramisu, p57 © *The Collection* by Antonio Carluccio (Quadrille)

Raspberry and tequila nieve, p40 © *Mexican Food Made Simple* by Thomasina Miers (Hodder & Stoughton)

We would like to thank Al Crisci and all our recipe contributors, and also Christopher Moore. Particular thanks to Alison Cathie, Ros Holder and Lucy Bannell, for the beautiful book they've put together. Very many thanks, too, to Alexandra Bertram.

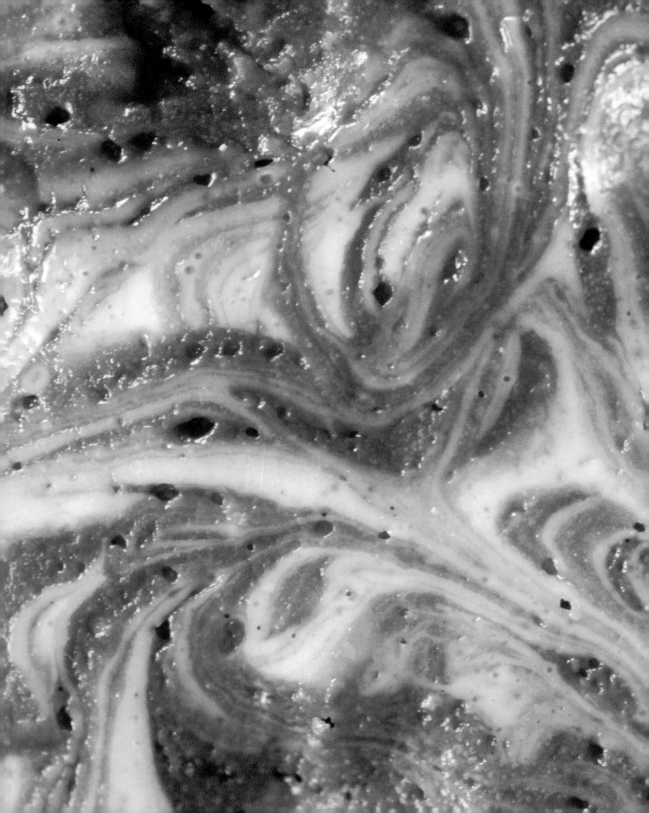